D0929322

yearBOOKS,INC.
Dr. Herbert R. Axelrod
President
Neal Pronek
Managing Editor
William P. Mara
Editor
David J. Zoffer
Assistant Editor
John Coborn
William P. Mara
Contributors

yearBOOKS are all photo composed, color separated, and designed on Scitex equipment in Neptune, N.J. with the following staff:

COMPUTER ART
Michael L. Secord
Supervisor
Stephen Beltle
Kenneth Bontz
Sherise Buhagiar
Patti Escabi
Sandra Taylor Gale
Pat Marotta
Joanne Muzyka
Robert Onyrscuk
Tom Roberts
Matthew Valenti

ADVERTISING SALES
George Campbell
National Manager
Amy Manning
Advertising Director
Jennifer Feidt
Advertising Coordinator
©yearBOOKS,Inc.
1 TFH Plaza
Neptune, N.J.07753
Completely manufactured in Neptune, N.J.

CONTENTS

An Introduction to TFH's Green Iguana Yearbook

EDITORIALLY SPEAKING...

Green Iguanas, *Iguana iguana*, have been immensely popular for decades. In the past, knowledge of their keeping requirements was very limited and resulted in the death of many thousands of specimens. Today, however, husbandry techniques have greatly improved. Photo by Jim Merli.

In the more industrialized nations of the world, the reptile-keeping hobby began growing during the period immediately following World War II. Today, this hobby is still on the rise (and stronger than ever, in fact). A statistic taken from a recent pet-industry survey suggests that almost three million households in the United States alone have at least one herptile pet.

In years past, severely limited knowledge of the requirements of captive reptiles led to the premature death of many hundreds of thousands, if not millions, of specimens. Often they perished simply because they were placed in climates so different from those of their native habitats. Fortunately, however, these early disappointments resulted in increased study of the welfare of these fascinating pets, and now there's no reason to expect them *not* to live long and happy captive lives.

The Green Iguana has been considered a standard herpetological pet for a long, long time. Green Iguanas are ideal subjects for anyone starting off in the lizard-keeping hobby. They are colorful, they tame fairly easily, they are relatively intelligent, and they can be trained to a certain extent. They often can be kept in apartments that are otherwise unsuitable for the more traditional pet such as a dog or a cat. They are not noisy and, if properly cared for, will not give off unpleasant odors. Specimens rarely are unavailable (it would be nearly impossible to find a reptile-oriented pet shop that didn't stock them), and they are relatively easy to feed.

This yearbook was specially prepared for people with an interest in Green Iguanas. There are facts useful to anyone with even the mildest curiosities—prospective keepers, armchair naturalists, curious beginners, seasoned hobbyists; the list goes on. We've presented it in a magazine format rather than in book form because books take time to produce properly, and during that production time information may become outdated as the wheels of research continue to turn, and new information comes to light. Periodical publications are more "timely," more "current," and ensure that you, the reader, be offered only the most reliable and up-to-date information available.

Put simply, the purpose of this volume is to enthuse and enlighten, accurately and efficiently. It is the publisher's sole wish that it does just that.

We hope you enjoy it.

Elementary Facts About Green Iguana

LET'S GET DOWN TO BASICS

A lot of "herpers" are familiar with the Green Iguana in captivity—how to feed it, how to house it, how to keep it clean—but not everyone knows basic facts like where it lives, how it lives, and so on. Let's take a closer look at some of the "fundamentals" of this most popular herptile.

DESCRIPTION

An adult Green Iguana is a pretty respectable-sized animal. A large male can reach a total (head, body, and tail) length of over 6 ft/182 cm, though the average adult length is more in the region of 5 ft/152 cm for males and a little shorter in females.

The robust body is laterally flattened (upright oval) in cross-section, a common characteristic of arboreal lizards. The head is relatively large and squarish, and the snout is rounded. The limbs are very powerful, the forelimbs being a little shorter than the those in the rear. There are five digits on each hand and foot, each tipped with a tough, sharp, and powerful claw. The tail, which comprises about 60% of the animal's total length, is thick at the base, tapering to a fine point at the tip. There is a long dorsal crest starting just behind the head, extending along the back, then stopping around the first third of the tail. The tallest spines in the crest are those on the nape of the neck. They may be up to 1

A main diagnostic feature of the Green Iguana is the group of large, roundish scales located just below the eardrum, which can be seen quite clearly in this photo (by Isabelle Francais).

in/2.5 cm high and sometimes are so heavy that they droop to one side. There is an extendable, laterally flattened, comb-edged dewlap under the throat and chin, this being larger and more conspicuous in the male than the female. The dewlap is extended with the aid of the hyoid bone, usually during territorial or sexual displays.

A particularly notable feature of the Green Iguana is a group of large, almost pearl-smooth scales located just below the conspicuous eardrum. In adult specimens, the largest of these scales may be over 0.5 in/1.2 cm in diameter. Notably, these scales are a diagnostic feature of the species when

distinguishing it from the only other member of the genus, the Antillean Iguana, *Iguana delicatissima* (on which the aforementioned scales are greatly reduced and the large "main" scale is absent). The scales on the Green Iguana's body are relatively small, being somewhat larger on the limbs and belly than on the back. The neck boasts a number of medium-sized conical scales while the head is covered with large, plate-like scales.

Adult Green Iguanas are green to gray-green in color, but some specimens may be bluish green, yellowish, or even orangish. The ground color is marked with a series of dark bands along the flanks and tail. Green Iguanas tend to darken with age, and some very old specimens may be almost black. The underside usually is a pale green to off-white. Experiments in selective breeding already have produced predominantly blue specimens, and it is quite possible that further color mutations will arise in the not too distant future. (Editor's

that these pores help to hold the cloacae in apposition during copulation.

Juvenile Green Iguanas are invariably a bright leaf-green color with few or no markings, although the site of the future dark bands may be tinged a turquoise blue. Also, juveniles have a poorly developed crest and dewlap.

Virginia Keys) and along the northeastern coast of Puerto Rico.

HABITATS

Although Green Iguanas occur over a large geographic area, they are very restricted in terms of habitat—they rarely stray far from permanent water. They live among the shrubs and trees where they feed upon buds, leaves, and fruits. When not active, they spend their time perched along branches that overhang the water. During the day they bask high in a tree canopy, maintaining their preferred body temperature of about 90°F/32°C by moving in and out of the shade. When night temperatures remain above 77°F/25°C, Green Iguanas spend their nights on a favorite "perch," but when the temperatures fall below this level they seek out a burrow or hollow limb, where they will rest in semi-torpor until the sun comes back up.

Young Green Iguanas do not possess the same striking crest on the head, and fan on the throat, that the adults do. Comparatively, young specimens look sort of "bald." Photo by W. P. Mara.

Note: Although unsubstantiated, there is a report of a single *albino* specimen that recently was sold for over $5000.00.)

The sexes are fairly similar, but the male is generally more robust, with a larger head, taller crest, and more prominent dewlap. The color and pattern may also be brighter and more pronounced, and there is a series of large femoral pores which are only vestigial in the female. It has been suggested

GEOGRAPHICAL RANGE

The Green Iguana occurs in suitable habitats from northern Mexico to South America (excluding a great deal of the Yucatan Peninsula) as far south as the Tropic of Capricorn in Paraguay and southeastern Brazil. It also can be found on a number of small islands off the Pacific Gulf and Atlantic coasts. It has been successfully introduced into the Miami and Fort Lauderdale areas of Florida (plus the Biscayne and

HABITS

When threatened by predators, Green Iguanas will drop from their perches (sometimes from a great height) into the water. Diving deeply, they hold their limbs against their body and "wiggle-swim," using their long, flattened tail for propulsion. They can remain submerged for several minutes at a time and often will do so until they feel all danger has passed. To be doubly safe, they prefer to resurface among nearby aquatic vegetation or tree roots rather than in a more open area, and even then they expose just enough of the head to look around. If they're not near enough to a water body when disturbed, they will drop to the ground, landing on all fours like a cat, then scuttle off at great speed and head either for water, ground cover, or another tree.

The long tail of the Green Iguana does more than help the animal swim—it also is used as an an organ of balance when climbing. Although the tail is not strictly prehensile (meaning "adapted for grasping and holding"), it can be used as a stabilizing or thrusting aid. As anyone who has had a lot of experience with angry Green Iguanas will tell you, the tail is also used as a weapon. Any sensible aggressor will think twice after experiencing the violent, whip-like action of the tail which, in large specimens, exerts considerable force (and inflicts considerable pain). Additionally, a threatened Green Iguana will not hesitate to use its strong jaws and serrated teeth as well as its sharp claws. Thus, large Green Iguanas should be treated with great respect, for they can do real damage to a human being (a good reason to spend time taming them when they're young!).

One more interesting function of the tail is something called *autotomy*. This is when the tail is voluntarily cast off because a predator has grabbed hold of it. Autotomy is utilized by many lizard species, some more readily than others. Green Iguanas use this method of defense only as a last resort. Such a situation may occur when the animal has taken refuge in a tree hollow and left part of its tail exposed. A predator applying pressure to the tail in an effort to pull the lizard back out is likely to end up with only a wriggling tail!

The tail of the Green Iguana has many purposes, the main ones being as a rudder to help the animal swim, as a balancing tool when it climbs, and as a whipping weapon of defense. Photo by Isabelle Francais.

Green Iguanas are seasoned tree-dwellers, where they may cluster in large groups to bask in sunlight or keep out of reach of predators. Photo by Isabelle Francais.

Miscellaneous Green Iguana Topics
ODDS AND ENDS

Who preys on Green Iguanas in the wild? Are there any stamps with Green Iguanas on them? How about conservation efforts concerning Green Iguanas? These are some of the topics discussed in this article.

as they emerge from the nesting burrows, hatchling Green Iguanas immediately make for the relative safety of nearby vegetation. During their swim to the mainland, island hatchlings have to run the gauntlet of predatory fish,

man is a potential enemy because Green Iguanas have been part of Native Amerindian diets for centuries.

It should be pointed out, however, that predators don't really have all that much of a negative impact on Green Iguanas because predation is a part of the Green Iguana's natural ecology. If anything, it was the colonization of Central and South America by Europeans back in the

Many people are unaware that there is a second species in the genus *Iguana—Iguana delicatissima*, also known as the Antillean Iguana. Due to its rarity, it is a perfect candidate for a captive-breeding program. Unfortunately, hobbyists are not allowed to keep it. Photo by Anita Malhotra.

GREEN IGUANA PREDATORS

Wild Green Iguanas, especially the highly vulnerable hatchlings, are preyed upon by a variety of creatures. In fact, one of the reasons Green Iguanas lay such a large number of eggs is so enough hatchlings will survive to produce a successive generation. Even

crocodilians, and turtles, and once on land they may be eaten by larger lizards, snakes, and mammals. Larger Green Iguanas also have to be careful of certain animals, such as anacondas, Boa Constrictors, caiman, eagles (and some other large birds), otters, bears, and jaguars (plus other "big cats"). Even

fourteenth and fifteenth centuries that rang the first bells of doom for the Green Iguana, not to mention many other native animal and plant species.

GREEN IGUANA CONSERVATION

The two major reasons for the demise of wild populations

of Green Iguanas are loss of habitat and pollution. Of course, not only the Green Iguanas are affected but *all* life in that particular area. As human populations grow and societies "modernize," the natural environment is transformed to suit human needs. Great tracts of vegetated land that once were ideal for Green Iguanas (and many other creatures) now are either under the concrete of

also take a toll. Roadways divide populations and create dangers for animals that need to cross over them. In time, after populations have become completely isolated from each other, the gene pool in one area becomes smaller and thus weaker.

In recent years, many conservationists have applied pressure on governments to preserve wilderness areas in order to prevent the

> *"Unless drastic measures are taken, we may see the extinction of vulnerable species such as the Green Iguana in a relatively short time."*

permit. Additionally, strict rules regarding the capture, restraint, transport, and ensuing care of specimens have been formulated.

The downside to this is that it is extremely difficult to enforce such regulations. While many countries have "jumped on the bandwagon" and adopted various internationally recognized conservation measures, their handling of these regulations leaves much to be desired. Some have designated certain areas as national parks and wildlife reserves in which the natural environment is maintained in pristine condition. But these areas are very small compared to those that continue to be deforested. Unless drastic measures are taken, we may see the extinction of vulnerable species such as the Green Iguana in a relatively short time.

One method of ensuring the continuing existence of Green Iguanas is to maintain sufficient breeding stocks in captivity. In fact, *all* keepers of Green Iguanas should make an effort to breed their animals. Apparently, a few "iguana farms" have been set up in countries where the Green Iguana occurs naturally, but, unfortunately, these farms are not so much for the conservation of wild populations as they are for profit from the lucrative trade in Green Iguanas as pets, mainly in North America and Europe.

The Antillean Iguana is native only to the southern Caribbean Islands. It differs from the Green Iguana mainly by having no large scale below the tympanum. Photo by Anita Malhotra.

the cities, are grasslands for grazing cattle, or are being used to cultivate commercial crops. Apart from the expansion of residential, industrial, and recreational areas, the increasing use of motor vehicles and the expansion of tourism creates further problems. Domestic animals such as dogs and cats

exploitation of vulnerable species. Green Iguanas are listed in the appendices of the Convention on International Trade in Endangered Species of Wild Flora and Fauna (known to most as CITES). This means the international trade of the species is allowed only under special circumstances and by special

Housing Techniques for Green Iguanas

A GREEN IGUANA'S HOME IS ITS CASTLE

An enclosure in which reptiles and amphibians are kept sometimes is referred to as a vivarium or a terrarium (plurals are vivaria and terraria). The modern trend is to use the latter word.

Terraria come in a range of styles and sizes and are built from a number of different materials. State of the art terraria often are made from fiberglass or plastic and sometimes are pre-equipped with all the necessary life-support systems.

The major prerequisites for a terrarium are that 1) it must be escape proof, 2) it must be easy to service, and 3) it must contain all the necessary climate-control components. A slightly less important consideration is the question of visual esthetics. For example, if you are going to have a large display terrarium, you naturally will want it to be

While Green Iguanas probably never will win any prizes for intellect, they are relatively smart for lizards. After a time they are able to recognize their owners and can be taught not to bite or scratch. Photo by Isabelle Francais.

Skull of a large male Green Iguana from South America. Photo by K. H. Switak.

The most common type of terraria are those made from glass.

tastefully decorated. However, esthetics are less important to someone like a breeder who has a large number of enclosures and doesn't have the time to decorate and then continually maintain each one.

GLASS AQUARIA

The most common type of terraria are those made from glass and can be purchased from just about any pet shop. These are suitable for Green Iguanas under the age of about 18 months. Due to the rapid growth and eventual large size of these lizards, aquarium tanks of a suitable size for subadults and adults will be quite expensive. For a pair of very small Green Iguanas, a glass tank of the "20-gallon" size will suffice. The tank must have a ventilated lid, and the lid should be tight fitting and secure. Screen-type lids will allow warmth and light to enter from any apparatus installed above.

HOMEMADE ENCLOSURES

To house very large Green Iguanas, many keepers build enclosures from timber and glass, the glass being used for the viewing panels. For one or two adult specimens, suggested dimensions are in the neighborhood of 6.6 x 3.3 x 3.3 ft/2 x 1 x 1 m (length x height x depth). This will allow one cubic meter of air space per animal, if you intend to keep a pair. Sizes suggested here are minimal, so if you can afford the space, make the enlosure even larger.

Homemade enclosures are best constructed from high-grade plywood of at least half-inch thickness. The boards should be screwed together, and the viewing panel can be made from a pane of glass fitted into a wood frame. This panel may be hinged or fitted into runners so it slides from side to side. Large doors should be hinged rather than fit into runners since they tend to warp and jam. There should be ventilation holes in each wall and in the ceiling, these being drilled with a "hole saw" and then covered with aluminum screening or hardware cloth.

All wood used should be sanded smooth and then primed, undercoated, and topcoated with a high-quality, non-toxic paint. This will protect it from moisture and to make it easier to clean. Alternatively, you could apply several coats of exterior polyurethane varnish. Yacht varnish, though expensive, will give a long-lasting waterproof finish.

To make cleaning chores a little easier, and to further protect the wood from moisture, you can fit an aluminum tray into the floor. The sides of the tray should be no less than 1 in/2.5 cm high so that the substrate is contained.

A ROOM ALL THEIR OWN

Some keepers hand over a whole room to their Green Iguanas, the room itself

Small Green Iguanas will be comfortable in 10-gallon glass tanks. Decor includes a simple substrate, a waterbowl, and some sturdy branches. Photo by Isabelle Francais.

becoming the terrarium. A room with a concrete or ceramic-tiled floor is best as it can easily be scrubbed and hosed down. A large water bath can be placed in the room and logs serviced by heat lamps will provide basking areas. Any heating pipes or radiators should be screened to prevent burns.

DRESSING THINGS UP

Decorations and furnishings are required to complete the interior design of any display terrarium. As with other herptiles, certain items work better with Green Iguanas than others.

Substrate Material: The terrarium floor should be covered with material that is easy to clean and change. I

have found pea-sized gravel to be the best choice for Green Iguanas. The nice thing about gravel is that it can be washed and reused. When doing this, place it in a large container (a bucket works well), wash it with soap and a little bleach, then rinse with a strong jet of water (such as from a hose) until the effluent runs clear. Finally, place the gravel out in the sun to dry. It is best to keep a spare quantity of gravel ready for immediate use so you can bed your Green Iguana's enclosure while the other is being cleaned.

Tree Branches: Being naturally arboreal, Green Iguanas rarely feel at home unless they have something on which to climb around. I have found a thick branch, with several other thinner branches, to be the most useful and visually esthetic. It

Organic substrates are ideal for Green Iguanas. Most are easy to work with, pleasing to the eye, and can be bought in bulk quantities. Photo courtesy of Coralife/Energy Savers.

is better use dead branches than cut healthy ones from a living tree. Many pet shops sell such branches. Make sure the branches you use are well-secured because you don't want them falling down while your Green Iguanas are on them! One method is to tightly wrap a branch with wire, then attach that wire to the terrarium wall.

Rocks: These are useful as decorative items, but they have other advantages as well. They often are used as basking sites and help keep a Green Iguana's claws trimmed. You should be able to find decorative rocks from pet shops. If not, you may have to go out and find your own. Be sure to get permission to remove any from private land. Like any other new items being put into an animal's enclosure, rocks should be thoroughly cleaned beforehand. They also should be placed securely so that they cannot fall over and harm the inmates. Groups of rocks are best cemented together to prevent accidents.

Plants: While placing live plants in a terrarium is okay when dealing with smaller lizards, doing this with Green Iguanas is very impractical. A Green Iguana will lay on them, dig them up, and sometimes even eat them! One compromise is to use artificial plants. Some very life-like and durable artificial plants are sold in pet shops. One decorating tip—do not clutter the terrarium. A simple arrangement involving only one or two plants often looks best.

Scenic Backing: Some hobbyists like to add feeling of depth to their animals'

terrarium by placing a scenic sheet on the back. Many scenes suitable for Green Iguanas are available in pet shops. Most sheets are reasonably priced and cut to fit most any tank.

Water Containers: The

A captive Green Iguana will fall victim to extreme stress if not given something to climb on. Remember that Green Iguanas are naturally arboreal, so they *need* to climb. Photo by Isabelle Francais.

choice ranges from cat litter tray or large dog bowl for small Green Iguanas, to a large dish basin or baby bath for adult specimens. A really dedicated enthusiast should consider building a small concrete pool complete with a drainage system. Whatever you use, the main criterion will be that the area is easy to service, bearing in mind that the water must be changed daily.

SCRUBBING AND POLISHING

In the interest of hygiene (and, in turn, the prevention of disease), it is important to

frequently and regularly clean the enclosure of your Green Iguana. The droppings of a healthy Green Iguana are fairly solid and can be removed from the substrate with a scoop. Substrate materials should be washed or thrown out and replaced (depending on the substrate in question) at regular intervals. About once per month you should give everything a thorough cleaning. Use hot, soapy water and just a touch of bleach, rinsing *very thoroughly* in cold.

About once per month you should give everything a thorough cleaning.

Getting a Green Iguana's Environment Right

SOME LIKE IT *HOT*

Green Iguanas can be filthy creatures, so you may find yourself frequently washing their enclosures. However, sanitation duties are a normal part of good husbandry and go a long way towards the control of diseases. Photo by Isabelle Francais.

Since captive Green Iguanas often are kept in climates that are alien to them, a keeper must provide environmental conditions that reflect those they are accustomed to. While many tropical animal species adapt fairly well alien climates, Green Iguanas usually do not.

Since the majority of Green Iguana hobbyists live in the cooler parts of North America and Europe (often called *temperate zones*), it is necessary for them to provide heated accommodation for their pets (although it may be possible to expose them to the outside on warm summer days).

There are many important factors to be considered with regard to the environment of captive Green Iguanas. The actual, physical components involved often are collectively called the life-support system, and without these components a Green Iguana will not survive for long. The main factors to be taken into consideration are temperature, lighting, humidity, and ventilation.

TEMPERATURE

Green Iguanas, like all reptiles, are *ectothermic*, meaning their body temperature is determined by their immediate environment. During the day, you should maintain the temperature of a Green Iguana's terrarium

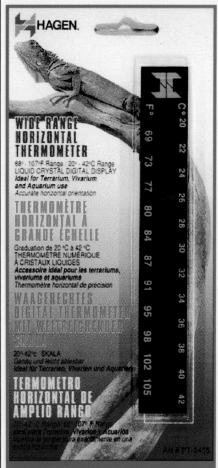

Keeping an eye on the ambient temperature of a Green Iguana's enclosure is an important facet of good husbandry. If the animal is allowed to become too warm or too cold, it could become ill. Fortunately, high-range thermometers designed specifically for herp-keeping are now available. Photo courtesy of Hagen.

somewhere in the range of 77 to 86°F/25 to 30°C. Additionally, there should be a basking area where your Green Iguanas can warm their bodies if they so desire. This area should be located at only one end of the enclosure so the inmates can move back to a cooler area if they need to/ want to. Prolonged exposure to temperatures higher than 95°F/35°C will quickly kill a Green Iguana (this sometimes being referred to as their

critical thermal maximum).

Another important thing to remember is that temperatures in the subtropics and tropics are almost always lower at night, so there should be a corresponding drop in your iguana's terrarium. Ideal nighttime temperatures are in the neighborhood of 65 to 71°F/18 to 22°C. If there is a danger of the temperature falling below this level, some form of subdued heating should be used.

The following is a discussion of some of the more commonly used heating components—

Ordinary Light Bulbs: In the past, ordinary incandescent light bulbs were the standard method of heating terraria. They often had to be left on day and night, forcing the inmates to endure both a constant (non-varying) temperature and

constant light. Though terrarium-heating techniques have advanced considerably since those days, ordinary light bulbs still have their uses. A low-wattage bulb placed inside an inverted flower pot makes an acceptable basking area for small Green Iguanas. Similarly, a low-wattage, red-colored bulb is an ideal for keeping the chill out of a terrarium on cool nights, and a blue bulb may give the impression of natural moonlight.

Heat Lamps: Various heat lamps can be used in a terrarium, some being made particularly for this use. Infrared lamps, of the type used in poultry brooders, can be useful. Suspending such a lamp over a large flat rock or a thick branch will give your Green Iguanas a nice basking area. You can control the temperature of this area by

Under-tank heating pads work well with Green Iguanas. They will warm only one particular section of the enclosure, giving the inmate more than one temperature zone to chose from. Photo courtesy of Hagen.

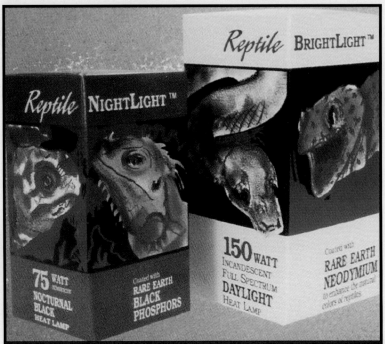

Bulbs designed specifically for the keeping of reptiles and amphibians now are available at many pet shops. Some, like those shown here, provide not only light, but a measure of heat as well. Photo courtesy of Coralife/Energy Savers.

raising or lowering the lamp. It is best to have the lamp *outside* the terrarium (aimed so its rays go through the screening) so there is no danger of the inmates burning themselves. There also are ceramic lamps which emit heat but no light, and can be used similarly.

Heating Pads, Cables, and Tapes: Flat, flexible, heating pads can be obtained in various sizes and should be placed beneath the terrarium where they heat up one section of the substrate (observe all safety precautions!). They are especially useful for tanks containing juvenile Green Iguanas.

Heat cables, of the type used by horticulturists, also can be useful in warming a substrate. The cable simply is buried beneath it (be careful with substrates that may be flammable).

Heating tapes are limited in application but, like pads, can be used to heat the bottom of a glass tank. They also are useful for providing supplementary warmth at night.

Hot Rocks: One of the most recent innovations made specifically for reptile keeping is the heated "rock." These are molded from fireproof material and contain an electric heating element that gets plugged into an ordinary outlet. One safety note—test a newly purchased "hot rock" before using it in the terrarium because defective models often overheat. Also, keep all heated rocks well away from water.

Aquarium Heaters: These can be used to keep the chill out of a terrarium's water body. Large bodies tend to cool quickly, creating a hazardous bathing area. A fully submersible aquarium heater, available at many pet shops, will alleviate this problem. Remember to keep it completely underwater (exposure may cause the unit to crack), and set its thermostat (most are built in)

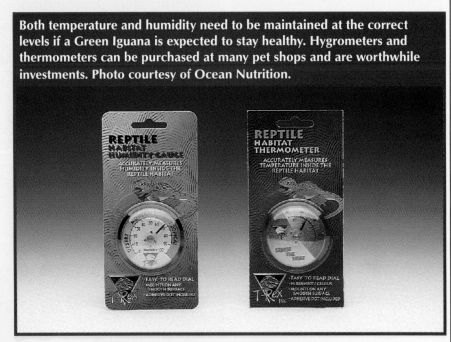

Both temperature and humidity need to be maintained at the correct levels if a Green Iguana is expected to stay healthy. Hygrometers and thermometers can be purchased at many pet shops and are worthwhile investments. Photo courtesy of Ocean Nutrition.

so the water temperature stays around 77°F/25°C.

Thermostats: Whatever kind of heaters you use, it is best to rig them up to a thermostat. The sensor should be placed in a position well away from any basking area so it will get a true reading. To be sure the thermostat is working properly, give it a trial run for 24 hours before you place any animals in the terrarium. If your animals require reduced night heating, it will be convenient to have two thermostats.

LIGHTING

There is much evidence to suggest that the health of Green Iguanas, plus other diurnal lizards, will deteriorate if they are denied natural sunlight, or a good substitute. Diurnal basking lizards require the ultraviolet rays of such light to help stimulate the manufacture of vitamin D3. One of the functions of D3 is its control over the actions of phosphorus and calcium in the body. A deficiency of vitamin D3 is likely to trigger various abnormalities in bone development, resulting in malformation.

A semi-outdoor terrarium with an opening in the roof obviously would be ideal for the provision of natural sunlight. Unfortunately, it is not as easy to obtain the same in an indoor enclosure. Sunlight through glass not only will heat up an enclosed space to a lethally high level but also will be filtered of all its valuable properties. You therefore must rely on an effective substitute.

Although there are no bulbs that provide *perfect* replication of natural daylight, there are some that come darn close. A few pet-product companies even market lights designed specifically for Green Iguanas (and other diurnal lizards). It will be to your benefit to shop around and see what's available. Whatever light you end up using, it is strongly advised that you follow the manufacturer's instructions, bearing in mind that some bulbs can burn a Green Iguana's skin should the animal get too close to them.

HUMIDITY

The humidity requirements of Green Iguanas are not completely understood. Green Iguanas can survive both in areas that have a more or less permanent high humidity and areas that have moderate or seasonal high humidity. Wherever they live, however, they rarely are far from a permanent water source. We therefore can assume that they are more comfortable in a humid environment than in a dry one. Indeed, too dry an environment is likely to result in a number of health problems.

Captive Green Iguanas can be kept in a semi-humid environment, which can be provided without too much trouble. One key is that the water body be large enough so that the animal can immerse itself if so desired. Heat in the terrarium will cause slow evaporation from the water's surface and in turn increase air humidity. If you want to experiment with humidity levels, you should invest in a hygrometer. You can increase humidity by misting the interior of the terrarium with a fine spray a few times each day, or put an aquarium airstone, attached to an airpump via some plastic tubing, into the iguanas' water body. This will agitate the water, in turn making a greater surface available for evaporation. Also, the bubbles will carry further moisture into the air.

In spite of the humidity

Providing your pets with the correct photoperiod (day/night cycle) is very important. Photoperiod is often a factor in determining a herptile's behaviorisms. Photo courtesy of Coralife/Energy Savers.

Keeping a Green Iguana in an outdoor enclosure is ideal if you have the space to spare. Outdoor enclosures should be tall, since the animals will want to climb (building a pen around a small tree is a clever approach), and should allow the occupants to receive direct sunlight. Photo by Isabelle Francais.

requirements, a Green Iguana's terrarium also must have dry surfaces. A specimen that is forced to lie on a wet surface for a long period could develop skin problems. In most cases, the provision of adequate basking areas will ensure such areas of dryness.

VENTILATION

It is important for stale air in the terrarium to constantly be replaced with fresh air, but the process must be somewhat controlled. Too much ventilation may cause drafts as well as a reduction in humidity, while too little will cause the air to become stagnant. Though the terrarium lid is likely to be screened, there should be a more ventilation holes (again, with screen coverings) cut through the enclosure walls. It is best to have these holes also covered with sliding hatches so the amount of ventilation can be adjusted when necessary.

SAFETY PRECAUTIONS

Remember that electricity is dangerous, especially when used in close proximity to water. Always use equipment of appropriate standard and ensure that all wiring is carried out correctly. If in doubt, go to the expense of hiring a qualified electrician. In the short run, it's more sensible than risking the health of both your animals and yourself.

Understanding the Green Iguana Diet

WHY DO THEY EAT THAT?

Many of the difficulties experienced by early Green Iguana keepers were diet related. Specimens often died from an inadequate diet or from secondary infections brought on by the same. It can be said that the provision of a balanced diet is one of the keys to keeping a captive Green Iguana healthy. Fortunately, nutritional studies have resolved many problems, but further research is required before we can say we have a complete solution.

Most of us understand what is meant by the phrase "balanced diet." To remain healthy and to function adequately, an organism must take in certain dietary constituents, and in sufficient quantities. These dietary constituents include the macronutrients (proteins, carbohydrates, and fats), which are required in relatively large quantities, and the micronutrients (vitamins and minerals), which are required in relatively small amounts but are no less essential.

Different animals have different diets. Reptiles, for example, require different dietary constituents than those of mammals and birds. At one time, canned dog or cat food was recommended as a major part of the Green Iguana's diet. Recent research, however, has shown that excessive quantities of these foods, designed primarily for mammals having high protein requirements, cause serious problems in Green Iguanas. You must, therefore, plan the diet of your Green Iguanas with care.

Let's take a brief look at the

Adding a dose of vitamin supplement to your Green Iguana's foodstuffs once every week is strongly recommended. Such supplements can be purchased at most pet shops. Photo courtesy of Coralife/Energy Savers.

various dietary constituents and their functions.

MACRONUTRIENTS

Proteins: These probably are the most important of the macronutrients. They are the building blocks of growth plus repair and regeneration of muscle and organ tissue. They play a part in other metabolic functions as well. Green Iguanas are efficient in processing vegetable-based proteins, which is good because too much animal-based protein can be bad for a Green Iguana's health.

Carbohydrates: These include sugars and starches and are common in vegetable material. Carbohydrates are required for the energy being burned in the muscles as the animal carries out its normal activities. Excessive carbohydrates are converted into fats.

Fats: These are stored in the tissues and can be converted into energy when necessary. They also act as shock absorbers. Excessive fat builds up in the tissues, causing obesity. Fats occur in both animal and vegetable materials.

MICRONUTRIENTS

Vitamins: These are organic substances required in relatively small amounts for the maintenance of various essential metabolic functions. Many animals, Green Iguanas included, are unable to synthesize most essential vitamins, so they get them through their diet.

The most important vitamins for Green Iguanas are A, B_1, B_2 complex, C (self-synthesizing), D_3, and E. A deficiency of vitamins, known as avitaminosis, can have serious consequences. Conversely, excessive amounts of vitamins, especially A and D_3, can be extremely debilitating. Vitamins are contained in many natural foodstuffs, but a keeper should supplement a Green Iguana's captive diet with a vitamin powder or liquid, just to be on the safe side.

Minerals: Various inorganic elements in the form of mineral salts are essential to the Green Iguana's diet in small amounts. The most important of these elements are calcium and phosphorus, which must not only be present in relatively large amounts but also must be available in the correct ratio.

Calcium is most efficiently absorbed from the intestinal tract when the calcium/phosphorus ratio is between 1.2:1.0 and 2.0:1.0 and sufficient vitamin D3 is present. Other important trace elements include sodium,

Calcium supplements also should be included in the diet of captive Green Iguanas. A lack of calcium can easily lead a Green Iguana to premature death. Photo courtesy of Coralife/Energy Savers.

The Foods of Captive Green Iguanas

WHAT'S ON THE MENU?

Carrots are among the many vegetables usually accepted by Green Iguanas. They can be offered whole, as shown here, but when shredded they are easier for the animal to consume. Photo by Isabelle Francais.

potassium, iron, magnesium, sulphur and iodine, copper zinc, manganese, cobalt, and selenium. Most of these are available in small but adequate amounts in a varied diet. However, calcium and phosphorus supplements should be given every now and then just to be on the safe side.

Green Iguanas primarily are herbivorous but will also take a small amount of animal material. It has been estimated that 80% of their diet consists of vegetable material (including shoots, leaves, and fruits) with the remaining 20% consisting of invertebrates, small vertebrates, and the occasional carrion. Hatchling Green Iguanas are more insectivorous than adults, their ratio of animal to vegetable food being about 50/50. The adult diet is realized at about 18 months of age.

Captive Green Iguanas do better if given a variety of foods rather than only two or three items. You will find that not all Green Iguanas will eat all the foods you offer. However, there is no harm in trying different items until a satisfactory diet has been determined.

Certain companies now produce canned foods for Green Iguanas (and other reptiles). These foods are supposed to contain all of the necessary constituents Green Iguanas need. However, if you decide to use them, it is recommended that you offer them only as part of a more varied diet or in an emergency situation where more preferable foodstuffs are unavailable.

The major part of a Green Iguana's diet should consist of greens chopped into bite-sized pieces (bearing in mind that greens offered in a dish do not provide the necessary resistance a growing plant does as pieces are torn from it). I have yet to come across a Green Iguana that is not crazy about lettuce, which is not necessarily a good thing since this vegetable has a rather low nutritional value. Therefore, lettuce should be given sparingly (as a treat perhaps). The leaves and flowers of the weeds dandelion (*Taraxacum*) and sow thistle (*Sonchus*) are nutritious and should be given in relatively large amounts whenever possible, plus those of *Hibiscus*. Also acceptable are rose petals, the leaves and fruits of Brazil cherry (*Eugenia*), the leaves and fruits of mulberry (*Morus* spp.), and the leaves, stems, and flowers of nasturtiums (*Tropaeoleum* spp.). Cactus pads and fruits, especially

The older a Green Iguana gets, the more herbivorous it will become. Young specimens have about a 50/50 ratio of plant-to-animal foods, whereas the same ratio for full-grown adults is around 80/20. Photo by Michael Gilroy.

those of prickly pear group (*Opuntia* spp.) usually will be taken. Other greens that can be tried include chopped cabbage (white and green), kale, spinach, broccoli, Chinese greens, alfalfa (including sprouts), clover, young grass stems, watercress, bean sprouts, and sprouting grains such as wheat or oats.

Recommended vegetables include raw carrots (grated),

Bananas may be accepted with great joy by Green Iguanas, but bananas should only make up a small percentage of their overall diet because their nutritional value is relatively low. Photo by Isabelle Francais.

pumpkin, sweet potatoes, cold cooked potatoes, peas in the pod (especially snow peas), okra, cucumber, tomatoes, and sweet capsicum.

Fruits should comprise only about 10% of the total Green Iguana diet. Apples, pears, peaches, cherries, plums, and mangoes all are acceptable. On a slightly lower nutritional level, bananas, strawberries, raspberries, blackberries, blackcurrants, grapes, oranges, and similar fruits

Pre-made foods designed specifically for Green Iguanas are now available at many pet shops. Such items make feeding very convenient for the keeper, and highly nutritional for the kept. Photo courtesy of Fluker Farms.

occasionally may be given as treats. Canned fruits also are safe. What should be avoided are any large seeds, for many contain prussic acid which, in sufficient amounts, can be debilitating or even fatal to a Green Iguana.

Experienced keepers probably have noticed that certain "human-food" items are eagerly accepted by Green Iguanas. From my experience, such items include fried rice, macaroni and cheese, spaghetti, quiche, pizza, apple pie, custard, and Black Forest cake. Though it may be quite amusing to see your Green Iguana tucking into a plate of chili, "people foods" should be considered taboo. They usually contain too much fat, leading the animal to obesity. Stick to the vegetables, fruits, and occasional animal foods.

Speaking of which, about 10 to 20% of your Green

Iguana's diet should consist of animal material. Lean hamburger may be given occasionally, as can lean minced chicken, pink mice, and chopped hard-boiled eggs. Canned dog or cat food was once a recommended part of the Green Iguana diet, but recent research has shown that they contain certain vitamins in excess of a

meadows, in woodlands, etc. With a large butterfly net or similar you can catch grasshoppers. Scoop up as many as you can and place them in a container with a ventilated lid. Non-hairy caterpillars also will be accepted, as will many kinds of beetles. Some Green Iguanas will eat cockroaches, but be careful that none

invertebrate food for insectivorous captive herptiles. Since those days, research has shown that the calcium/phosphorus ratio of mealworms is inadequate, and mealworms therefore should be used as only a small part of the the diet.

You can purchase mealworms from most any pet shop, for reasonably low prices, and in bulk quantities. They can be maintained in shallow trays (plastic shoeboxes with holes drilled through the lids for ventilation are ideal). A 2-in/5-cm layer of a bran/oatmeal mixture is placed in the tray, this being used as both food and burrowing substrate. A swatch of cloth is placed over the bran/oatmeal substrate, and a couple of pieces of fresh potato, apple, or carrot are placed on top to provide moisture. Do not put the

Pre-made Green Iguana foods sometimes are offered in convenient meal-sized cubes and can be offered on a daily basis. Check with your local pet shop for the availability of such foods. Photo courtesy of Ocean Nutrition.

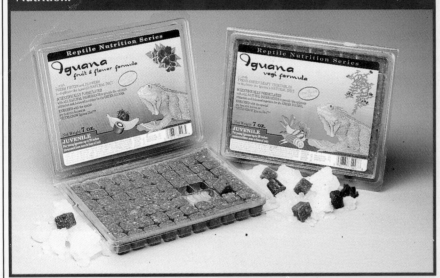

reptile's requirements. Green Iguanas given cat or dog food will develop mineralization of the tissues, which eventually will be fatal. Though small amounts given every now and then will do no harm, it is better to stay on the safe side and altogether leave out such foods.

Try to make invertebrates the main part of the animal part of a Green Iguana's diet. Hatchling and young iguanas will be very keen on these items. In temperate areas, during the summer months, you will be able to collect many livefoods. Good spots to go include your garden, in

escape into your house!

If you are unable to collect livefoods, there are several commercially cultured livefoods available. These include mealworms, waxworms, and crickets, all of which usually will be taken by Green Iguanas (at the very least by young specimens). You either can buy small quantities of these items at regular intervals or, to save money (and frequent trips), buy them in bulk and house them.

Mealworms: These are the larvae of the Flour Beetle, *Tenebrio molitor,* and were at one time the most-often used

Many keepers like to hand-feed their Green Iguanas, feeling it develops a stronger bond between them. Photo by Isabelle Francais.

vegetables/fruits *in* the substrate because they will rot and can spoil the whole culture.

Crickets: Crickets undoubtedly are the most frequently offered food for insectivorous herptiles. Like mealworms, they can be bought from pet shops, in bulk, and for low prices. They are a source of high nutrition for Green Iguanas. Though there are many species, the two most commonly cultured

Beware! Green Iguanas will gladly accept a lot of foods that are bad for them, like the macaroni seen here. Many such foods are loaded with fat and sodium and will be a detriment to your pet's health! Photo by W. P. Mara.

One way to increase the nutritional value of crickets is to place them in a small plastic bag and sprinkle in a little calcium powder. Shake the crickets until they are covered with the calcium "dust," then offer them to your iguanas. Photo courtesy of American Reptile.

are those of the genera *Gryllus* and *Acheta*. Purchased quantities can be kept in small containers with pieces of corrugated cardboard or old egg boxes as hiding spots. A small bowl containing a piece of wet cotton wool or a moistened sponge will provide drinking water, and bran or oatmeal along with a small amount of fresh vegetables or fruits will provide the food. A container of damp sand or vermiculite should be provided for gravid females so they

have a place to lay their eggs. These egglaying containers should be removed (and new ones put in their place) every week or so, then placed in a separate container so the hatchlings will be safe, i.e., not eaten by the adults. If kept at a temperature of about 79°F/26°C, the eggs will hatch in about three weeks. The newly hatched nymphs will be about .12 in/3 mm long (like small ants!), and with adequate feeding they should grow to adult size (about 1/in 2.5 cm) in around six weeks.

Locusts: Not easily found in

A Green Iguana that you know to be a little "snappy" can be fed via forceps. Photo by Isabelle Francais.

pet shops, locusts usually have to be obtained from specialist suppliers. Nevertheless, if you have the chance to get them, do so, for they are quite nutritious. Adults grow up to 3 in/7.5 cm in length, making them ideal for larger Green Iguanas. Locusts can be fed a mixture of bran and crushed oats supplemented by fresh greens. Long grass stems are a convenient green food. They can be kept fresh by placing the stems in a bottle of water with wadding packed around the neck to prevent the insects from falling in and drowning. Locusts are best kept at a temperature of about 82°F/ 28°C in a tall, well-ventilated aquarium. Plastic trays containing about 3 in/7.5 cm of moist sand should be placed on the floor of the enclosure so the gravid females have a place in which to lay their eggs. Once the eggs are laid, move the egglaying containers into a separate accommodation so the eggs can hatch in safety. The tiny hatchling locusts can be given the same diet as the adults.

Buying large Green Iguanas has one main advantage–you can breed them. On the other hand, large specimens also need a lot of enclosure space and plenty of food. Also, ill-tempered adult specimens can be difficult, and sometimes dangerous, to deal with. Photo by U. E. Friese.

What Do I Need to Know?

GETTING YOUR FIRST GREEN IGUANA

Obtaining a Green Iguana is an exciting event. It's hard to miss the joyful look in one's eyes as they walk out of a pet shop proudly carrying a "critter box" or a ten-gallon tank with all the environmental components in place and the lizard already inside.

FIRST, THINK ABOUT THIS...

It's important to remember that any animal kept in captivity is totally reliant upon its keeper. A Green Iguana kept in a glass tank is unable to search for food or water and cannot avoid overheating or overcooling in adverse captive conditions. It therefore is imperative that you be vigilant in providing the correct diet and environment. You'll need to prepare food, check life-support components, and keep accommodations clean. All of these chores will take time out of your day, so don't become a Green Iguana owner if you don't have such time to spare!

Another factor to take into consideration is that many Green Iguanas are acquired when they are very young (and very cute). Indeed, it is better to buy a young specimen, which you can tame and train, than a boisterous subadult or adult who is "set in his/her ways" to the extent that the meanness cannot be "trained out of it." Unfortunately, some people buy a young Green Iguana *only* because it is cute looking, not taking into account the fact that it will one day be about six feet long and need a lot of space! Also, don't take up Green Iguana keeping until you have weighed all the pros and cons and discussed them with other members of your household. Although you might be crazy about Green Iguanas to the point of fanaticism, the people you share your house with may not be quite as enthused!

WHEN MAKING YOUR PURCHASE...

Having made the decision to keep a Green Iguana, your first step will be to prepare its enclosure. Don't go out and get a Green Iguana first and then start worrying about this later on. The poor animal will be stressed in some unsuitable container while you're getting things sorted out!

The best place to go for

Choosing a Green Iguana requires a little bit of knowledge and a lot of good judgment. Learn about what you're getting (and getting into) before you lay your money down. Photo by Jim Merli.

Green Iguana specimens is a pet shop. If at all possible, try and get captive-bred specimens. Doing this means one less specimen has been taken from the wild. Also, a captive-bred specimen will settle into a captive environment better than one that is used to wild living.

Make sure the dealer you obtain your specimens from is reputable and keeps the animals in prime condition. It is a mistake to buy animals from premises that are dirty and untidy, keeping in mind that *all* pet shops suffer from a certain amount of filth. The trick is to know how much filth is *too* much.

It is important that you buy healthy animals from the outset; you certainly won't want to be making a series of veterinary calls once you get the animals home. If you are a beginner, it would be wise to take an experienced hobbyist with you when you are purchasing your first specimen. If you join a local herpetological club, there is sure to be somebody there who'll give you advice.

Again, select only healthy specimens, i.e., those that are alert, bright-eyed, and plump. Their skin should be clean and unblemished, with no lumps or wounds (well-healed scars usually are no big deal). The limbs should operate smoothly and there should be no swellings on the digits or the joints. Make sure there is no discharge from the mouth or nostrils. Ask if the animal is feeding well and on what. You should continue the same diet when you get the animal home, but if you consider the diet unsuitable, gradually change it.

When shopping for a Green Iguana, take into account the quality of the surroundings in which the specimen is kept. Filthy enclosures are a breeding ground for all sorts of nasty diseases, many of which will infect not only the Green Iguana you buy, but also those that the new animal comes in contact with, i.e., *the rest of your collection.* Photo by W. P. Mara.

BRINGING THE IGUANA HOME

Once you've purchased a Green Iguana, it's important that you get the animal home and into its new quarters as soon as possible. Captive reptiles suffer the most stress when they're being transported.

The best type of container is a cloth bag. Each specimen should have its own bag to avoid the possibility of them accidentally injuring each other. The bags, tied at the neck, can be placed in a cardboard or wooden box for extra safety and insulation.

In the absence of a cloth bag, a cardboard box can be used, but make sure it is secured with plenty of tape. I

once had quite a shock in my car when I had placed a poorly secured cardboard box on the rear seat. During the journey, a medium-sized Green Iguana jumped up on my shoulder! In cold weather, it is wise to place bags or boxes in a larger insulated container. It goes without saying that livestock should never be left in a parked car during excessively hot or cold weather.

THE IMPORTANCE OF QUARANTINE

There always should be a period of time in which you keep new livestock separated from animals you already have. Keep the new ones under observation for about three weeks before introducing them to the others. Quarantine quarters (preferably set up in a separate room) should be kept simple. An aquarium tank or a glass-fronted box with a newspaper substrate, a hiding place, a waterbowl, and a climbing branch will suffice. Naturally you must supply the necessary warmth and lighting. If the iguana seems healthy after the three-week term, you can introduce it to your other stock with confidence.

Every inch of a Green Iguana that you are thinking of buying should be closely inspected. Look for signs of burns, scars, open wounds, ticks, mites, and a number of other subtle things. Photo by W. P. Mara.

When picking up a Green Iguana, be sure to give it as much bodily support as possible. If you don't, the animal may thrash about violently and give you nasty scratches and bites. Also, holding a Green Iguana will tell you something about its state of health. Healthy specimens will struggle to get away (even tame specimens will squirm a little), whereas ill specimens will put up virtually no resistance because they don't have the strength. Photo by Isabelle Francais.

Green Iguanas that were frequently handled when small grow into real "pets" that you can carry around or rest on your lap. Photo by Isabelle Francais.

Handling, Taming, and Training

THE GREEN IGUANA AS A FRIEND

Though it is quite easy to handle small Green Iguanas, large specimens are a different kettle of fish, especially those that have been wild-caught or have grown up without much handling. In general, Green Iguanas do not like being handled, but with training they can get used to things like being perched on your arms or shoulders. A young Green Iguana being held for the first time will be squirmy and uncooperative, so you need to know the proper way to restrain it. You should place your hand over its body and then gently but firmly grasp it with your fingers. Grip it well but not tight enough to injure it. With practice, your technique will improve.

Once you start handling your Green Iguana, keep doing it on a regular basis so the animal remains tame. Always be gentle, moving your hand slowly towards the animal and only making a grab if it attempts to scuttle away. Each time you pick up the animal, apply a little less restraint then the last time; eventually the animal will allow you to lift it without a struggle. However, keep in mind that sudden movements or loud noises are likely to send it scuttling for cover in spite of how tame it seems to be.

Here's a handling story that may prove useful to some of you concerning keeping Green Iguanas in close proximity with other animals—I once had a large pair of Green Iguanas that I had raised from fairly small juveniles. They had been given to me as a birthday present when I was serving in the armed forces in Germany (where, incidentally, Green Iguanas are very popular). On leaving the army, my wife and I stayed in Germany for a while and became proprietors of a bar that was popular among members of the armed forces of NATO. Of course, the Green Iguanas, now quite large, came with us and were kept in a large terrarium in our living quarters. We handled both of them regularly. The female (who we named Iris) always remained nervous while the male (named Big Ig) became remarkably tame and docile.

Sometimes, on quiet afternoons, I took Big Ig into the bar and introduced him to some of our customers, most of whom were quite amused by his presence. He would parade along the bar, stopping now and then to taste the counter top with his large, pink tongue. Customers would eagerly give him a sip of their beer or offer him a cocktail cherry, the latter being munched on with obvious pleasure.

Handling a Green Iguana as much as possible is strongly advised. Large specimens that are not accustomed to the human touch will be nasty and irascible and have the potential to cause deep scratches and bites. Photo by Isabelle Francais.

(Editor's Note—It is strongly urged that you *not* offer any of your herptiles beer or any other alcoholic beverage since the effects of such on reptiles and amphibians is largely unknown.)

One customer regularly brought his dog into the bar. The animal normally would lay quietly at the customer's feet next to the counter, then the day came when Big Ig stuck his head over the edge of the counter and was spotted by the dog. The dog took a leap towards him while letting out a series of sharp yelps. In his fright, Big Ig turned and leapt from the bar onto the display shelves and, while clambering to the top, knocked bottles of liquor all over the place. As I ran alongside him, catching a flask of rum here and a bottle of vodka there, the customers burst into a state of hysteria, some of them falling off their stools with laughter. Not thinking the situation quite so funny myself, I eventually caught hold of Big Ig and returned him to his enclosure. From then on, he was taken into the bar only on very special occasions, and then only after I was sure there were no dogs present!

Although I was once introduced to a Green Iguana that would regularly take a ride on a collie's back, the moral of the story is that Green Iguanas generally should not be mixed with other pets because you never can be really sure what will happen.

Green Iguanas in excess of 2 ft/60 cm that have had little or no handling can pose problems. They have strong, sharp teeth and may well attempt to use them. Their claws also are quite powerful, and, perhaps worst of all, they can whip their tails with remarkable accuracy. In such cases, the best course to take is to handle them as little as possible (now you can understand why it's so important to start handling them when they're young). When they do need to be restrained, it's best to wear heavy gloves. Grip the animal with one hand around its neck, restraining its front forelimbs with your fingers. With the other hand, grip its abdomen just in front of its hind limbs, and finally, tuck the rear part of its body under your elbow in order to restrain the rear limbs and the tail.

Having just mentioned the tail, I should stress that a Green Iguana should never be lifted by this appendage. Like many lizards, a Green Iguana can shed part or most of its tail as a mechanism of defense (a practice known as *autotomy*). I once had an escaped Green Iguana wedge itself behind a radiator and had to remove it quickly before it burned itself. Having no better means at my disposal, I decided to pull the animal out by the tail. Sure enough, the tail broke off in my hand,

If for no other reason, small Green Iguanas make the best pets because they are so "manageable" in this stage of life. If you handle them every day (or, at the very least, every few days), they will grow accustomed to you. Photo by Isabelle Francais.

Only a Green Iguana that has been handled since birth could rest so peacefully on its owner's shoulder. Photo by Isabelle Francais.

Due to the enormous popularity of Green Iguanas, some companies now offer interesting accessory products. Two of these are the "biker jacket" and the "comfort leash," the latter enabling you to actually take your Green Iguana for a "walk." Photo courtesy of Ocean Nutrition.

leaving the poor iguana with a bloody stump. I eventually managed to extract the reptile with the aid of a broom handle, and after some veterinary treatment it was returned to its enclosure. In time the tail grew back, but it was considerably shorter, and uglier, than the original.

Finally, some mention should be made of the idea of taking a Green Iguana for a "walk," i.e., take it outside on a leash-type of restraint in order to give the animal some fresh air. The line of the leash is attached to a special body harness designed to fit around the thorax (some companies actually make such items; check with your local pet shop). It does a Green Iguana a great deal of good to get outside in the fresh air and sunlight when the weather is suitable, such time being when the air temperature is over than 85°F/25°C. Since Green Iguanas are unpredictable in temperament, it is wise to keep them on their "leash" at all times. (although never leave one tied up and unattended because the animal may become inextricably entangled and hang itself). A loose specimen may very well disappear up a nearby tree if you are not vigilant. One of my own once scaled my backyard fence and went up one of my neighbor's trees. It took all afternoon and a lot of hassle in front of an ever-increasing audience to get him back down!

Always make a point of handling a Green Iguana by the head and the body, not the tail. A Green Iguana's tail can snap off if submitted to enough pressure. Photo by Isabelle Francais.

Breeding Green Iguanas in captivity can be difficult in the sense that the breeder needs to provide the animals with plenty of room. In fact, those who do propagate this species almost always house their specimens in outdoor pens. Photo by Isabelle Francais.

Green Iguana Reproduction in the Wild

GREEN IGUANA LOVE

Unless you can afford captive-bred adults (which almost always are very expensive), your Green Iguana breeding stock should consist of specimens obtained when they were very young and then raised in captivity. Such specimens make ideal breeders. Photo by Isabelle Francais.

The more northerly ranging populations of wild Green Iguanas mate in the fall. During this time, the males will be even more territorial than usual. A dominant male will control a patch of land containing a few trees and several females. Vagrant males, often younger and smaller, may approach in an attempt to impress the females and perhaps get a chance of mating. The dominant male usually takes a high position on a tree or a rock so he can view most of his territory. On spotting a challenging male, he will approach it in a threatening manner, standing high on his legs, inflating his body, curving the back, extending his dewlap, and sometimes opening his mouth and hissing. He will turn flank towards the intruder in an attempt to appear as large as possible, and bob his head. The intruding male may be so intimidated with the display that he will become submissive, lowering his body to the ground and turning away in retreat.

A more aggressive intruder, however, may respond by making a similar display of boldness. This is when a small war begins. The pair will circle each other warily for a few moments, then clash by banging their heads together. The weaker individual will eventually turn away in retreat. It should be noted that most of these fights are purely ritual, and the animals are rarely injured.

It seems that these confrontations are the dominant males' stimulus to mate; the more frequently he has to defend his territory, the more sexually active he becomes. Copulation begins as such—the male approaches a female with head bobbing and an erect dewlap. If receptive to these advances, the female will take the submissive position. The male will then seize her in his mouth, usually at the nape of the neck, and hold up her tail with one of his hind legs so he can bring his cloaca into apposition with hers. Male Green Iguanas possess a pair of hemipenes, but only one is used during copulation. This hemipenis is inserted into the female's cloaca so that spermatozoa can be injected. Copulation may take anywhere from 15 to 45 minutes (sometimes less, but only rarely). A non-receptive female, or one that is already gravid, may take on an aggressive stance or scurry off.

The eggs are laid after 50 to 90 days. The gestation time may be influenced by environmental factors such as temperature, humidity, and the availability of food and water. Eggs normally are laid at a climatically favorable time, i.e., during a time of optimum temperature and humidity. About one to three weeks before laying, the female will stop feeding but will take in increasing amounts of water. Then she'll begin seeking out nesting sites. These sites may be some distance away from the female's normal living area. Gravid females may swim out to little islands in rivers and estuaries to lay their eggs in areas safe from predators and human egg collectors. Sunny, moist, sandy banks just above

the high water mark are the most preferred spots. If there is a shortage of such sights, the females may struggle for "land rights."

Burrows are excavated in the sand using the front limbs, with the rear limbs used to kick back the excavated soil. The burrow usually is 3 to 6 ft/1 to 2 m long with a broad egg chamber at the end. The female turns in the nest chamber and lays her eggs, usually two at a time. It may take three to six hours for all eggs to be laid. Average clutches contain 20 to 40 eggs, but as many as 70 and as few as eight have been recorded. Eggs average about 1.33 in/3.4 cm in length, 0.94/2.4 cm in diameter, and 11.5 gm in weight. The eggs are white and have a soft but

Getting Green Iguanas to copulate can be tricky, but once you succeed, the pair in question should not be disturbed. Photo by John Ramsay.

Only the healthiest specimens should even be considered as part of a breeding program. Photo by Isabelle Francais.

"After all of the eggs are laid, the female leaves the burrow and carefully fills it in before returning to her normal place of residence."

tough parchment-like shell. Young females may lay fewer and smaller eggs than more mature specimens. After all of the eggs are laid, the female leaves the burrow and carefully fills it in before returning to her normal place of residence.

Incubation time varies with temperature and humidity, but at 86°F/30°C, and with good humidity, incubation should last around 100 days. At hatching time, a neonatal Green Iguana (8 to 11 in/20 to 28 cm in length) will slit open its shell using its *egg tooth*, which is located just under the tip of the snout and falls off shortly after hatching. Eggs often hatch concurrently, and the newborns, after digging their way to the surface, may migrate in large groups to nearby feeding areas. They may remain in these groups for days, foraging and even sleeping together among low foliage. They will feed on a mixture of vegetable and animal material and grow rapidly, usually reaching sexual maturity in the third year of life.

The moment every breeder waits for—a healthy neonate squirming out of its shell. Even at this time, a keeper should not attempt to handle the newborns. Wait until they are *completely free* of their eggs before attempting to pick them up. Photo by K. H. Switak.

Breeding *Iguana iguana* in Captivity

HOW TO MAKE YOUR OWN GREEN IGUANAS

Although Green Iguanas are being captive bred in greater numbers than ever before, there still aren't enough offspring to satisfy the commercial demand. Thus, wild specimens are still collected on a regular basis, causing real trouble for a species that already is growing rarer and rarer.

It therefore is very important that Green Iguana hobbyists make every effort to breed their specimens, bearing in mind that every home-bred specimen means one less taken from the wild. You do not have to own a lot of Green Iguanas in order to do this; by cooperating with other hobbyists, you can get mating pairs together just as many dog owners do.

Any Green Iguanas that you suspect to be gravid (pregnant) should be placed in an enclosure of their own (or with other gravid females) and left undisturbed. They particularly should not be handled. Photo by Isabelle Francais.

(cautiously; you don't want to become a casualty of the battle) and put him back in with his original female. It is important to avoid allowing the combat to get to the stage where one of the males becomes the "loser." If you time it just right, both males will believe they have "won" and will proceed to mate with their respective females. Whatever the outcome, at least one of the males will be ready to go, and that's certainly better than nothing.

Some breeders like to go through this procedure several times to ensure a viable mating. Once the female is gravid (obvious increase in girth), it is best to remove her from the male and place her in her own enclosure.

HOW TO "GET THEM GOING"

Several factors decide the successful breeding of captive Green Iguanas. First of all, they must be of breeding age (sexual maturity is reached in three to four years). Climatically, a reduction of photoperiod from 12 hours of light per day to eight, plus a reduction in temperature of a few degrees for a couple of months in the fall, is required.

As we know from the mating behavior of wild Green Iguanas, the mating urge in

the male is increased through competition with other males. If you keep two pairs of Green Iguanas, it is possible to fool both males into thinking they are victorious, thus rendering them "ready to mate." Remove one male from its enclosure and introduce him to the pair in the other. This will make the second male defensive and territorial, and the "intruding" male will retaliate accordingly. As soon as both have reached the combat stage, you can remove the intruding male

TAKING CARE OF THE EGGS

The gravid female should be provided with slightly moistened sand in which to burrow and lay her eggs. If possible, the sand should be at least 12 in/30 cm deep (deeper if possible). If the sand is too shallow, there is a possibility the mother will damage some of her eggs while trying to bury them.

About two to three weeks before egglaying commences, the female may cease feeding. You should still provide food

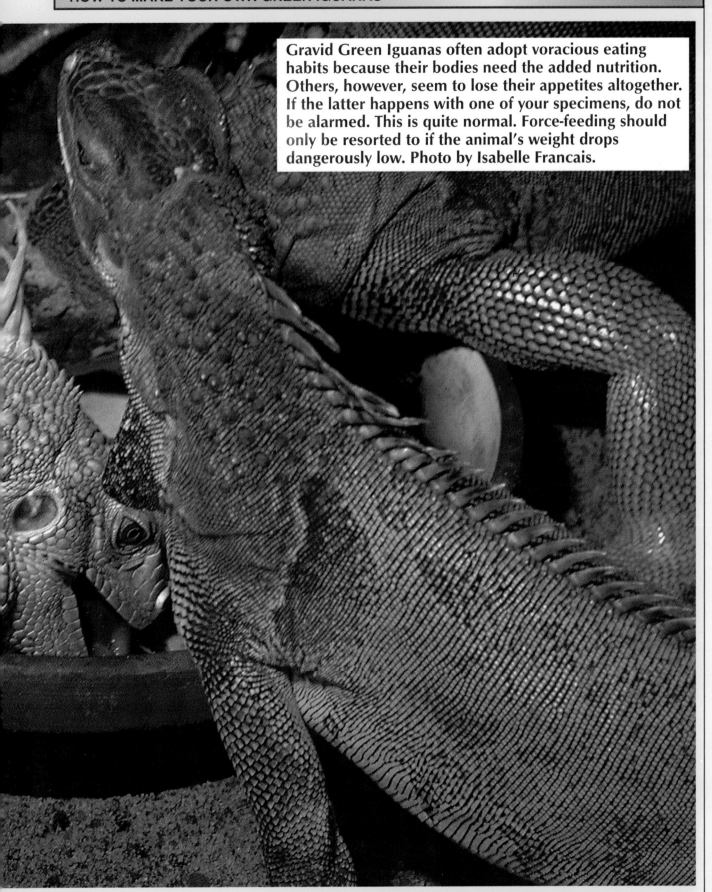

Gravid Green Iguanas often adopt voracious eating habits because their bodies need the added nutrition. Others, however, seem to lose their appetites altogether. If the latter happens with one of your specimens, do not be alarmed. This is quite normal. Force-feeding should only be resorted to if the animal's weight drops dangerously low. Photo by Isabelle Francais.

in case she changes her mind. Also, she will take in a lot more water than usual, so always have that available too.

When egglaying time is close, the female will become increasingly restless, wandering around the terrarium, testing the substrate with her tongue, and pushing her snout inquisitively into the corners. Hopefully she will use the egglaying site you have provided, but sometimes she will ignore it and lay the eggs exposed, scattered, in a clump, or in the waterbowl.

There are some very good commercially manufactured incubators available, but most hobbyists prefer homemade versions. Often used is a plastic shoe or sweaterbox (probably the latter when you consider the large number of eggs in the average Green Iguana clutch) with a few small holes drilled through the lid to allow for air circulation.

The container also has to be bedded with some type of incubation medium. Several types have been tried, but the best two are vermiculite and sphagnum moss (or a

buried in neat rows to about three quarters of their depth, leaving the last quarter exposed so they can be inspected.

The eggs will absorb moisture from the incubation medium, which you need to keep damp by checking it every other day and mist-spraying with lukewarm water (*around* the eggs, not on them) when necessary. As the embryos develop and more moisture is absorbed, the eggs will fill out and increase in weight. Infertile eggs will not absorb moisture, but don't discard *any* eggs until you are sure they have spoiled. An ideal incubation temperature is 77°F/52°C.

If all goes well, the eggs will hatch in 90 to 120 days. This waiting period can be maddening for an eager keeper. Sometimes you may even be tempted to open an egg to see if an embryo really is developing. Don't! You might destroy the only viable egg in the clutch! When eggs are opened prematurely, the embryos almost always die. Disturb the eggs as little as possible, and leave them in the position in which they were laid; there is no need to turn them as you would turn birds' eggs. Any eggs that you know for sure are bad are likely to turn moldy and pale. Such eggs should be discarded so the mold doesn't spread to the good ones.

Young Green Iguanas always should have food available. The first few years of their life will be the most important in terms of growth. Photo by Isabelle Francais.

You must be alert at this time, ready to collect the eggs as soon as they've been laid and place them in an incubation container. Needless to say, the eggs need to be dug up very *carefully*.

Since conditions in the terrarium usually aren't favorable for egg incubation, you must move the eggs to a separate incubation container.

combination of the two—eggs buried in the vermiculite with slightly moistened moss draped around them). Vermiculite, in case you don't know, is an inert, sterile, absorbent material used both for insulation and in the horticultural industry. It should be moistened to the point where it is damp, *not soggy*. The eggs should be

THE BIG DAY

When they are ready to leave their eggs, the hatchlings will slit through the shells with their egg tooths. There may be several lulls in this activity as the babies rest between efforts to free themselves. It can take quite a few hours before hatching is complete, so be patient. Sometimes a particularly weak hatchling just won't make it. If one is having obvious difficulties, you can slit the shell a little more with a small pair of sharp scissors or a razor knife, but be careful not to damage the yolk sac (or the animal, of course). Sometimes the fluids will dry out as the youngster is hatching, causing it to adhere the shell. This problem can be helped by mist spraying or by gently dabbing around the area with a piece of wadding soaked in lukewarm water.

DEALING WITH THE LITTLE ONES

Once the hatchlings have left the shell and are freely moving about, they should be removed from the incubator and placed in nursery accommodations. By this time, the yolk sac, which is

> ## "Sometimes a particularly weak hatchling just won't make it."

(full-spectrum light) at all stages of life, but they particularly need it during their early years. One way to cut down on lighting costs is to have one long bulb shining into a number of enclosures (overhead, through the screen tops).

Enclosures for newborn Green Iguanas should be kept simple. A few climbing branches, an easy-to-clean substrate, some hiding places, and a good-sized water body will suffice. Photo by W. P. Mara.

> ## "Functional nursery enclosures can be large plastic containers or 10-gallon glass tanks with screen tops."

attached to the belly, will begin to dry up. Once it's gone, there will be a tiny scar. Functional nursery containers can be large plastic containers or 10-gallon glass aquariums tanks with screen tops. It is best to have only two hatchlings per enclosure. Each should contain a shallow water bath and offer high humidity.

Newborn Green Iguanas require unfiltered sunlight or good quality artificial daylight

Hatchlings should be fed a mixture of finely chopped greens (clover, romaine lettuce, spinach, hibiscus leaves, etc.), a little chopped fruit, some finely shredded carrot, and a little lean mince. One or two crickets, mealworms, or other suitably sized insects can be offered daily. And finally, a little bone meal combined with a vitamin/mineral supplement should be sprinkled over the food twice per week.

Close Relatives of the Green Iguana

FRIENDS AND FAMILY

There has been a major change in the classification of the family Iguanidae. Before this change, the family contained some 700 species in about 60 genera. Now it has been been split into no less than eight families, with only eight genera being left behind. These cover the larger and more familiar iguanids. It is worth taking a brief look at some of them in case a hobbyist wishes to expand his or her interests beyond the ever-popular Green Iguana.

GENUS *AMBLYRHYNCHUS*

MARINE IGUANAS
Bell, 1825

The single species in this genus is the Marine Iguana, *A. cristatus*. It is one of the most remarkable iguanids in that it is the only one that regularly takes to salt water. It is found only on the Galapagos Islands, these being located in the Pacific Ocean about 600 miles off the coast of Ecuador. Marine iguanas are protected and thus rarely seen in captivity other than in major zoos. This is just as well since providing a suitable environment for them would be extremely difficult. Reaching a total length of 69 in/175 cm, these robust creatures have a long, paddle-like tail used to propel them through the water as they search for their staple diet of algae and seaweed. The snout is short and rounded, and there is a saw-like crest extending from the neck to the tail. Ground color normally is dark gray, but breeding males exhibit patches of bright red. Spending much of their day basking on the coastal rocks and cliffs (often in large, crowded groups), they enter the water at low tide to browse on submerged vegetation. Interestingly, these animals have developed special nasal glands that help them excrete excessive salt taken in with the diet.

GENUS *BRACHYLOPHUS*

FIJI IGUANAS
Wagler, 1830

The two species in this genus often are collectively known as the Fiji iguanas (although they also occur on the Tonga Islands). Individually, they are known as the Banded Iguana, *B. fasciatus*, and the Crested Iguana, *B. vitiensis*. Why they occur so far away from their closest relatives (in Central and South America) still remains a mystery, though "rafting" (floating on some buoyant natural object) followed by further evolution seems to be a highly plausible explanation.

Both species reach a maximum length of around 39 in/100 cm and superficially resemble the Green Iguana in basic body shape. They occur in tropical forests and are about 90 % herbivorous, the remaining 10% of the diet being smaller vertebrates. The coloration of both species is similar—bright green with broad pale green to white bands. *B. fasciatus* has a very short dorsal crest, while that of *B. vitiensis* is markedly taller. Displaying males can darken their body pigment to almost black.

These are considered by many to be the most colorful and attractive members of the Iguanidae, but, unfortunately, they are heavily protected by environmental law. Still, specimens do occasionally

The Marine Iguana is virtually never seen in captivity, even in zoos, because it is such a difficult animal to both house and feed. The bulk of its diet consists of kelp and marine algae. Photo by William B. Allen, Jr.

appear on the market. Their husbandry is very similar to that of the Green Iguana.

GENUS *CONOLOPHUS*

GALAPAGOS IGUANAS
Gray, 1831

The two species of Galapagos iguanas, *C. subcristatus* and *C. pallidus*, are protected by environmental law and therefore unavailable to most hobbyists. Both species are similar in appearance. *C. subcristatus* reaches about 43 in/110 cm in length, of which

Both Fiji iguanas, *Brachylophus* spp., are protected by environmental law and thus cannot be kept by private collectors. This is rather a shame because they are among the most attractive of all iguanids. Shown is the Banded Iguana, *B. fasciatus*. Photo by R. D. Bartlett.

In spite of the fact that the Fiji iguanas are off limits to private collectors, the few zoos that keep them report they do quite well. They are very hardy, accepting a wide variety of food items, and have a fairly even disposition. Photo by R. D. Bartlett.

The Galapagos iguanas, *Conolophus* spp., are another highly protected iguanid group. Like their close relative the Marine Iguana, they are native only to the Galapagos Islands, where they are almost exclusively herbivorous. Photo by K. H. Switak.

"The Fiji iguanas are considered by many to be the most colorful and attractive members of the Iguanidae..."

about half is tail. The compact body is furnished with strong limbs. There is a high crest on the neck, and a shorter one along the back that runs to the base of the tail. The basic color is more or less a uniform yellowish brown, sometimes with a little red on the sides and limbs. These iguanids inhabit dry, rocky inland areas, feeding on cactus and some grasses.

Most Galapagos iguanas are dully colored, usually some shade of brown with hints of yellow. Some specimens, however, boast a little red on the sides and limbs. Photo by R. G. Sprackland.

There are only two species of the Galapagos iguana—*C. pallidus* and *C. subcristatus*. The latter is depicted in all three photos on this page. Both species are similar in appearance, and both reach a length of about 43 in/110 cm. Above and below photos by R. Wallace.

GENUS *CTENOSAURA*

BLACK IGUANAS or SPINY-TAILED IGUANAS
Wiegmann, 1828

Commonly known as Black or Spiny-tailed iguanas, this genus contains almost a dozen species, including former members of the genus *Enyaliosaurus*. They all are native to various parts of Mexico and Central America and inhabit open woodland and rocky areas, where they often take cover in crevices. All have rows of enlarged spines around the base of the tail, making it an effective weapon.

The best-known species in the genus probably is *C. pectinata*, a native of Mexico that has been successfully introduced into parts of southern Texas and southern Florida. It sometimes is available through the pet trade. Reaching a maximum length of 48 in/121 cm, it has a raised dorsal crest that is more prominent in males. The hatchlings are green, and the adults are gray, brown, or yellowish, with darker but poorly defined crossbands. *Ctenosaura* specimens require a fairly large terrarium with basking spots warmed to around 104°F/40°C. Naturally, cooler spots also should be available, and the temperature should be reduced during the night (to around 70°F/21°C). Specimens feed on a variety of both plant and animal material (although they are primarily herbivorous).

Formerly a member of the genus *Enyliosaurus*, *C. defensor* is one of the most colorful spiny-tailed iguanas. Photo by R. D. Bartlett.

"All spiny-tailed iguanas have rows of enlarged spines around the base of the tail, making it an effective weapon."

Members of the genus *Ctenosaura* are native to Mexico and Central America, where they live in woodlands and rocky areas. Photo of *C. quinquecarinatus* by R. D. Bartlett.

"Ctenosaura specimens require a fairly large terrarium with basking spots warmed to around 104°F/40°C."

Like most lizards, the tail of a spiny-tailed iguana can break off fairly easily. Notice the length of regenerated tail on this wild specimen. Photo by W. Wuster.

Ctenosaura sometimes shows up for sale in the pet trade. Specimens need plenty of climbing space, and males shouldn't be kept together since they are so territorial. Above, *C. pectinata*. Photo by R. S. Simmons. Below, *C. similis*. Photo by Michael Cardwell.

Spiny-tailed iguanas are primarily herbivorous. Young specimens may take certain insects in their diet, but the adults feed mainly on plant material. Vitamin supplements are recommended for captive specimens. Shown is *C. palearis*. Both photos by R. D. Bartlett.

There are about six species in the genus *Cyclura*, and the most common in the herpetocultural hobby probably is the Rhinoceros Iguana, *Cyclura cornuta*. Members of this genus are among the more terrestrial iguanids, but young specimens may take to the air once in a while. Photo by Paul Freed.

GENUS *CYCLURA*

RHINOCEROS IGUANAS
Harlan, 1824

Collectively, these are known as the rhinoceros iguanas. They are native to the Antilles, and six species usually are recognized. One of the best known is the Rhinoceros Iguana, *C. cornuta*. Reaching a total length of around 39 in/100 cm, it is a heavily built creature with a relatively large head (especially on the males) that boasts a pair of bulbous swellings on the crown. The three short horns on the snout (which are comparatively shorter in the female) are what inspired the common name (plus the fact that some angry specimens often seem as bellicose as a miffed rhino!). There is a dorsal crest running from the neck and to the base of the tail, and the ground color of the dorsum is pretty much uniform dark gray to olive, with darker (although vague) crossbands sometimes being present.

Rhinoceros iguanas live in open woodland areas, often taking refuge in pre-dug burrows. They are becoming scarce in the wild due to loss of habitat and predation (including human). Captive specimens require a spacious area (preferably a full-room terrarium) with an air temperature of around 79°F/ 26°C and a local basking spot warmed to around 95°F/35°C. Temperatures should be reduced at night to around 68°F/20°C.

Though mainly herbivorous, Rhinoceros iguanas will take their share of animal foods.

"Though often considered herbivorous, rhinoceros iguanas will take their share of animal foods."

These include dead mice, day-old chicks, lean meat (in moderation), and eggs. Rhinoceros iguanas repeatedly have been bred in captivity, especially in zoological collections, but further efforts are required if we are to save this magnificent creature from extinction. At the risk of sounding dramatic, there seems to be very little hope for this animal in its native habitat.

Ricord's Iguana, *Cyclura ricordi*, a native of Haiti, is another ground iguana occasionally seen in the hobby. It is longer and more slender than *cornuta*, reaching about 48 in/120 cm in total length. Notably, it lacks the horns on the snout. Its captive care is similar to that of *C. cornuta*.

**TOP: Skull of *Cyclura cornuta*. Photo by Ken Lucas.
CENTER: Rhinoceros iguanas have been the focus of many captive-breeding programs, particularly in zoos. Photo by R. G. Sprackland.
BOTTOM: One of the rarer rhinoceros iguanas, *Cyclura nubila lewisi*, from the Grand Cayman Islands. Photo by K. H. Switak.**

Apparently, rhinoceros iguanas are not all that difficult to breed, even for the private enthusiast. It should be noted that many species are becoming scarce in the wild, so if you have the opportunity to breed any, do so. Shown is *Cyclura nubila*. Photos by Michael Cardwell (above) and Bill Christie (below).

GENUS *DIPSOSAURUS*

DESERT IGUANAS
Hallowell, 1854

This genus contains three species, two of which are confined to small islands in the Gulf of California and are rarely available in the pet trade. The third and best-known species is simply called the Desert Iguana, *D. dorsalis*, and is native to the arid and semi-arid regions of southwestern USA and Mexico. A diurnal, basking creature, it rapidly takes refuge in burrows or thick vegetation when disturbed. With a maximum length of 16/40 cm (half of which is tail), the Desert Iguana has a relatively small, rounded head

The genus *Dipsosaurus* contains three species, but two are confined to small islands in the Gulf of California and are never seen in the pet trade. The third, *Dipsosaurus dorsalis*, shown here, is often seen in private collections. Photo by W. P. Mara.

Although not often bred in captivity, the Desert Iguana makes a good captive and can be propagated with little difficulty. The young have a diet that most keepers can provide with ease. Photo by R. D. Bartlett.

Unlike many other iguanids, desert iguanas don't have an obvious crest on the head. Also, they are the smallest iguanids, adults reaching only around 1 ft/0.3 m. Photo by R. D. Bartlett.

Notably, desert iguanas need it very hot in captivity—their basking area, warmed via a "spot lamp," should be somewhere in the neighborhood of 103°F/39°C! Photo by Ken Lucas.

and a compact body. There is only a suggestion of a dorsal crest, and the long, tapering tail is covered with keeled scales. The color is grayish brown with darker bands, which lighten considerably when the lizard is basking, making it appear almost white.

This species frequently is kept by hobbyists, only thriving if given high daytime basking temperatures (to the tune of 104°F/40°C!), low humidity, and faithful full-spectrum lighting. The opportunity for specimens to move into cooler areas also must be provided, plus a nighttime reduction in temperature to around 68°F/

20°C. A medium-sized terrarium is suitable, and only a small waterbowl is necessary. Artificial "burrows" in the form of lengths of plastic piping pushed diagonally into a deep and sandy substrate will provide adequate shelter. Desert iguanas feed on a variety of plant matter, including dandelion leaves and flowers, clover, some fruit, and some animal material. Newly captured specimens may be reluctant to feed until given the leaves of pungent herbs such as sage and rosemary.

GENUS *SAUROMALUS*

CHUCKWALLAS
Dumeril, 1856

The status of this genus remains uncertain. Up to seven species have been

The Desert Iguana is becoming more and more popular with hobbyists, which is easy to understand considering its hardiness. The only problem a keeper may encounter is with recently caught adults, who may stubbornly refuse most foods. Photo by Michael Cardwell.

Desert iguanas like to spend a bit of time underground, and one clever way to accommodate them in captivity is to push short sections of plastic piping into the enclosure substrate. Photo by K. H. Switak.

The Chuckwalla, *Sauromalus obesus*, is the best known member of its genus, at least among hobbyists. It grows to about 18 in/45 cm and requires a basking spot of about 103°F/39°C. Photo by Isabelle Francais.

Chuckwallas are clever creatures when it comes to defense and escape. When threatened, they will jam themselves into a crack or crevice and inflate their bodies, making it virtually impossible for a predator to extract them. Photo of *S. varius* (above) by Michael Cardwell. Photo of *S. hispidus* (below) by R. D. Bartlett.

suggested, but some authorities regard a few of these only as subspecies. The best-known form, among hobbyists anyway, is simply named the Chuckwalla, *S. obesus*, which grows to 18 in/45 cm. This creature might humorously be described as a pot-bellied lizard due to its rotund body. There are loose folds of skin around the neck and shoulders, the head is broad, and the tail is thick at the base and has a blunt tip. There is no dorsal crest. The male has a black head, forelimbs, and thorax. Females and juveniles usually are crossbanded dull yellow and gray. Wild Chuckwallas usually live in rocky areas and, when disturbed, will wedge themselves into narrow rock crevices by inflating their bodies, making it almost impossible for a collector to remove them without causing injury. Chuckwallas are exclusively herbivorous and thus should be given a variety of plant material. The housing, temperature, and lighting requirements are as described for the previously discussed *Dipsosaurus dorsalis*. Artificial rock crevices can be made by using some flat slabs separated by rounder stones. (make sure everything is secure so the whole structure doesn't crumble down and injure the inmates).

Chuckwallas are almost exclusively herbivorous (the young may take some small invertebrates), making them easy to feed. A variety of vegetable matter, along with a small dose of multivitamin powder, makes a good diet. Of course, you shouldn't be afraid to try other items as well (fruits, grasses, etc.). Photo by George Pisani.

Setting up a chuckwalla enclosure is fairly simple. The key word is *dry*. A substrate of sand (or a mixture or sand and gravel), with a few large rocks (preferably flat ones), and high heat offered via a "spot lamp," will suffice. Photo by Paul Freed.

The chuckwallas are native to the southwestern United States and northern Mexico. They seem fairly calm and curious, but, like most lizards, do not like to be handled. Photo by K. H. Switak.

HOUSING

GENUS \ CATEGORY	SIZE OF ENCLO-SURE (FOR ONE ADULT)	IDEAL SUBSTRATE	HOURS OF FULL-SPECTRUM LIGHTING PER DAY
AMBLYRHYNCHUS	5^Wx5^Hx2.5^D ft / 1.5^{W}x1.5^{H}x.75^D m	Gravel	7 to 10
BRACHYLOPHUS	3^Wx3^Hx1.5^D ft / 0.9^{W}x 0.9^{H}x .45^D m	Dry Sandy Soil	7 to 10
CONOLOPHUS	3^Wx3^Hx1.5^D ft / 0.9^{W}x0.9^{H}x.45^D m	Sand and/or Gravel	7 to 10
CTENOSAURA	4^Wx4.5^{H}x1.5^D ft / 1.2^{W}x1.35^{H}x.45^D m	Sand	7 to 10
CYCLURA	4^Wx4^Hx2^D ft / 1.2^{W}x1.2^{H}x6^D m	Dry Soil or Sand	7 to 10
DIPSOSAURUS	3^Wx3^Hx1.5^D ft / 0.9^{W}x0.9^{H}x.45^D m	Sand and/or Gravel	7 to 10
IGUANA	6^Wx6^Hx3^D ft / 1.8^{W}x1.8^{H}x9^D m	Sand and/or Gravel	7 to 10
SAUROMALUS	3^Wx3^Hx1.5^D ft / 0.9^{W}x0.9^{H}x.45^D m	Sand and/or Gravel	7 to 10

FEEDING

GENUS \ CATEGORY	MOST COMMON FOODS (ADULTS)	MOST COMMON FOODS (JUVENILES)	PERIOD OF TIME BETWEEN MEALS
AMBLYRHYNCHUS	Kelp, marine algae.	Kelp, marine algae.	Day or two
BRACHYLOPHUS	Mostly plant material, plus some insects.	Even amounts of plant material and insects.	Two to three days
CONOLOPHUS	Mostly leafy greens and grasses; they love cactus.	Grasses, leaves, some soft fruits.	One full day
CTENOSAURA	Mostly plant material, plus some insects.	Mostly insects.	Two to three days
CYCLURA	Vegetables, fruits, insects, etc. Highly omnivorous	Willing to accept many things. Try a number of different items.	Two to three days
DIPSOSAURUS	Mostly plant material, but will take some live food as well.	Small insects and soft fruit.	One full day
IGUANA	Mostly fruits and vegetables, very little live food.	Even amounts of plant material and insects.	Day or two
SAUROMALUS	Plant material. Occasionallly some small vertebrates.	Plant material. Occasionally some small vertebrates.	Two to three days

HOUSING

IDEAL TEMPERATURE	HUMIDITY LEVEL	CAGE DECOR	SUGGESTED METHOD OF HEATING	MISC. COMMENTS
90's (°F). Lowered at night	Low to Moderate	Many large rocks	Ambient	Difficult animal to house—requires a large marine water body
85 to 88°F with a very small reduction at night	Moderate	Branches, rocks, and a few large plants	Ambient	Very arboreal animal. Do not neglect the need for branches
90's (°F)	Low	Many rocks and a few large branches	Likes to bask, so use a heat lamp	Needs a large water bowl and will drink from it often
93 to 105° F with a reduction to the mid-70's at night	Low	Rocks and branches	Ambient, or by the use of a Hot Rock	*Ctenosaura* are avid climbers, also, the males are very territorial
82 to 95° F with a drop to around 77° F at night	Low	Medium-sized rocks and some driftwood	Hot rock plus ambient	Mostly terrestrial, although young specimens climb occasionally
93 to 105° F with a drop to around 75° F at night	Low to Moderate	Rocks, branches, and some plants when keeping the southerly ranging species	Likes to bask, so use a heat lamp	Beware of over-heating and assure nightly temperature drop
82 to 100° F during the day, and 68 to 77° F at night	Moderate to High	Many large branches for climbing	Ambient	Will spend most of their time off the ground
93 to 105° F during the day, dropped to around 80° F at night	Low	A few large rocks	Likes to bask, so use a heat lamp	Keep males seperated. Provide shelter by piling rocks into small caves

FEEDING

BEST TIME OF DAY TO FEED	WILLING OR UNWILLING FEEDERS?	SUPPLEMENTS	TREATS	MISC. COMMENTS
During daylight hours	Willing	Vitamin powder sprinkled on food once per month.	N/A	Food items may be very difficult to aquire.
During daylight hours	Willing	Vitamin powder, sprinkled on food once every two weeks.	Soft fruits	These iguanids drink droplets from leaves and do not need a water bowl.
During daylight hours	Usually willing, but can be stubborn	Occasional light sprinkling of vitamin powder.	Cactus	Sensitive specimens can be thrown from their feeding routine very easily.
Day or night	Usually willing, but can be stubborn	Specimens that are not very carnivorous should have vitamin powder every two weeks.	Small crabs, fruits, and meat	Seems to take many items not associated with iguanids, so you can experiment.
During daylight hours	Willing	Strips of raw beef with some vitamin powder sprinkled on.	Rice, breads, some commercial foods are okay	Willing to eat a great many things. Beware of obesity.
During later daylight hours	Willing	Small bits of raw beef with some vitamin powder sprinkled on.	Large arthropods	A willing feeder that will do well with a well-balanced diet
During daylight hours	Willing, but new specimens may be stubborn	Vitamin powder on all foods every two weeks.	Miscellaneous items, but avoid those that are overly fatty	After a while, *Iguana* specimens will eat just about anything.
During early daylight hours	Willing, but many specimens need privacy	Vitamin powder on all foods every three weeks.	Insects, if they will take them	Sensitive animals that usually don't enjoy being watched as they eat.

BREEDING

GENUS \ CATEGORY	HIBERNATION	NUMBER OF EGGS PER CLUTCH	LENGTH OF EGGS
AMBLYRHYNCHUS	No	Around 3	Around 1.6 in / 4 cm
BRACHYLOPHUS	No	3 to 6	Around 1.6 in / 4 cm
CONOLOPHUS	No	Around 10	Around 2 in / 5 cm
CTENOSAURA	No	15 to 50	Around 1.1 in / 2.8 cm
CYCLURA	No	10 to 20	Around 2.8 in / 7 cm
DIPSOSAURUS	Yes (mild)	3 to 10	Around 1.1 in / 2.8 cm
IGUANA	No	30 to 50	Around 1.6 in / 4 cm
SAUROMALUS	Yes (mild)	5 to 15	Around 1.4 in / 3.6 cm

NATURAL HISTORY

GENUS \ CATEGORY	AVERAGE ADULT LENGTH	RANGE	NATURAL BREEDING SEASON
AMBLYRHYNCHUS	To 5.77 ft / 1.75 m	Galapagos Islands	December to January
BRACHYLOPHUS	To 3 ft / 90 cm	Fiji and Tonga Islands	Mostly in November
CONOLOPHUS	To 3.3 ft / 1 m	Galapagos Islands	August to October
CTENOSAURA	To 3 ft / 90 m	Mexico, Central America, and Panama	March to April
CYCLURA	To 4 ft / 1.2 m	Antilles	Variable and very short
DIPSOSAURUS	To 1ft / 1.2 m	Southwestern U.S., nothern Mexico, and some small islands	April to May, and sometimes in the autumn
IGUANA	To 6.6 ft / 2 m	Central Mexico to Central South America, and a few Caribbean Islands	October to December
SAUROMALUS	To 1.5 ft / 45 cm	Southwestern U.S. and northern Mexico	March to April

BREEDING

IDEAL INCUBATION TEMPERATURE	LENGTH OF INCUBATION	SIZE OF HATCHLINGS	SUGGESTED FOOD FOR HATCHLINGS	MISC. COMMENTS
82 to 86° F / 28 to 30° C	Between 100 and 120 days	Around 5 in / 12.5 cm	Marine algae, mashed kelp	Almost all captive breeding of this genus occurs in zoos.
75 to 81° F / 24 to 27° C	Between 160 and 170 days	Around 3.2 in / 8 cm	Small insects, soft plant and fruit material, all mashed	In the wild, incubation time is remarkably long: up to 35 weeks.
82 to 86° F / 28 to 30° C	Between 90 and 110 days	Around 4 in / 10 cm	Chopped and mashed fruit	Apparently not difficult to breed, although mostly done in zoos.
82 to 86° F / 28 to 30° C	Around 90 days	Around 2.4 in / 6 cm	Soft-bodied insects, mashed soft fruits	Could be a good captive if more domestically bred specimens were available.
Around 84° F / 29° C	Between 160 and 190 days	Around 7 in / 18 cm	Insects, soft fruits, and finely chopped meats	This genus needs to be bred more in captivity. Wild numbers are becoming critically low.
82 to 86° F / 28 to 30° C	Between 85 and 110 days	Around 1.9 in / 4.9 cm	Insects and soft fruits. Some leafy material	Not hard to breed in captivity, but not done often.
Around 86° F / 30° C	Around 85 days	Around 2.8 in / 7.0 cm	Finely cut bananas, carrots, and lettuce, plus some insects	Breeding these requires a great amount of space.
Around 86° F / 30° C	Between 85 and 110 days	Around 2.2 in / 5.5 cm	Plants, leafy greens, small insects. All mashed	Breeding seems to take a particularly heavy toll on the females of this genus.

NATURAL HISTORY

PROTECTED STATUS	DISPOSITION	GENERAL FARING IN CAPTIVITY	RECOMMENDED PURCHASE SIZE	MISC. COMMENTS
Internationally protected	Calm, but objects to handling	Poor	N/A	Virtually never kept, except in zoos. Captive needs very difficult to provide.
Internationally protected	Fairly calm	Fair. Very delicate	N/A	Rarely seen in private collections. Some zoos breed them.
Internationally protected	Bold and wary of humans. Will bite	Good	N/A	Interest in captive breeding these has steadily grown.
Still obtainable by hobbyists	Most specimens will bite viciously	Fair. Should only be kept by experienced hobbyists	1 ft / 30 cm	Common, but they do not make great pets.
Internationally protected: populations declining	Fairly calm, but can defend itself very well if it chooses	Good	N/A	Almost never seen in captivity. Becoming very rare.
Some species are still obtainable by hobbyists	Alert and quick to flee	Fair	0.5 ft / 15 cm	Does okay in captivity but seems very adverse to human company.
Currently listed in Appendix II of CITES	Fairly calm and can be tamed	Good	2.5 ft / 75 cm	Most captive specimens are still coming from the wild.
Some species are highly protected	Calm, but objects to handling	Good	.75 ft / 22.5 cm	Legally obtainable species are very popular in the hobby and do quite well.

A wild adult Chuckwalla, photographed by R. D. Bartlett in the southwestern United States.